Motherhood on the Wisconsin Frontier

By Lillian Krueger

ABELGIAN mother told her son that as a young woman she trudged at times from her wilderness home in Granleigh, a crossroad settlement—now called Lincoln—in Kewaunee County, to the mill at De Pere, carrying a sixty-pound sack of wheat. At three o'clock in the morning she set out on the sixty-mile round trip, arriving at the mill at about six o'clock in the late afternoon. With the other girls who came to the mill she was given permission to sleep on gunny sacks in the engine room, where it was warm. The next day she was homeward bound with the precious bag of flour, thinking nothing of the heavy burden. "It was considered a vacation of a sort. . . . It was a change of motion!" commented her son. At least now the family no longer received its sustenance from the Belgian overlord in lieu of wages, so the change of motion was good.[1]

The two Polish Kazmerchak brothers while grubbing, plowing, and seeding their newly acquired Kewaunee County lands, retained an indelible picture throughout the years: their Polish master leaning gracefully against his stone fence in old world Pudewitz—a cluster of houses on a large estate—watching them prepare their farm garden plot. Side by side Walentin and Steve pulled the clanging drag, not having had the courage to ask the master for his idle horses, too. "The fellow stood there and watched us—watched us so impersonally—well, we felt like a couple of animals!"

That's what started them for America, where there was no master staring at them while leaning against his stone fence.[2]

The young German housewife, who helped pile up and burn the brush on a Green Lake County farm, had seared into her mind the nights she spent as a child poaching faggots on a great estate at the German-Polish frontier. There was so little wood in the cottage. And now she was living on a forested farm where faggots and even logs were being burned to make place for the first harvest.

Economic advantages were not the only attractions that beckoned people to America. Among the early arrivals there were those who could not forget their regimentation into the state church, others their conscription into the army. Though these racking pictures had an insistent way of suddenly flashing back, there were some who possessed no plaguing memories: theirs had become a look of contentment after the earlier years of impatience and longing, faces which plainly expressed the simple Finnish proverb, "One's own cabin, one's own freedom." The beginnings of a dream come true.

The innate sense of the rightness of things, largely shared by the waves of immigrants, made mountains into molehills and overlay the great frontier terrain with an uprising optimism. In retrospect the aspect is forbidding peaks and crags; but to the young immigrant fathers and mothers it was a great adventure, and their bridges were

[1] This incident is contained in a letter in the author's files written by Lee W. Metzner, Casco, Wisconsin, August 10, 1945.

[2] Lee Metzner, "Polish Pioneers of Kewaunee County," in the *Wisconsin Magazine of History,* 18: 273-274 (March, 1935).

A young Chippewa Valley family, about 1885.

burned with their tearful farewells to the old folks. Those who had long traveled the "road of endurance" often did not attempt the new trail.

This is the story of one phase of the Midwest immigration, the story of the frontier mother. Her courage, initiative, and ingenuity, though tempered by loneliness and fear, contributed in full measure to a region's birth; with no thought of self, her doing has become an epic of the American way of life. Lest we forget, and the upcoming generation learns too little about her hard-earned glory, this part of Wisconsin's frontier history, centering in the 1840's and 1850's is here retold.

The mother arrived in the Middle West from the Old World, from the seaboard, particularly from the New England and New York regions, or from the states intervening. Her infrequent letters were written to her native Scandinavia, Poland, Germany, England, or Ireland, often requiring many months to reach the old home; sometimes they took the slow route to Vermont, New York, Ohio, or Indiana. Upon reaching the Promised Land her husband, if discriminating and able, probably chose lands situated on a lake or stream or containing a spring. Wells were costly and not easily obtainable, and a water source was carefully sought. If he chose oak openings—an interspersing of meadow and forest—the building of the log

cabin and the planting of the first crop were greatly simplified.

The wilderness home could be occupied within a few days, a few weeks, or after several months, depending upon its size, sturdiness, and comfort, but the description of a log cabin without the mention of snow sifting onto the attic floor and over the beds is rare indeed. Sometimes the mother remained with her children at the city of debarkation while the father and the men in his group left to look for farms in the hinterland. A very simple shelter might be built at once, and he then returned to move the members of his family in an ox- or horse-drawn vehicle to their new home.

The makeshift dwellings, when the family immediately accompanied the father, must have been amusing sights. A Rock County Norwegian family lived in a haystack for three months, and surely their completed cabin must have had a feeling of real permanence, if not elegance, about it. At times a mother's duties were carried on in and around the wagon in which they jolted to their "home," or it may have been in a crude brush shelter hastily put together. She considered herself very fortunate if she could live in the cabin or barn of a relative or friend who had preceded her to the Middle West and whose homesteading was somewhat advanced.

The first English colonists did not build the log

*This family was living on a farm on county road X, a quarter mile east of the Trout Run
Methodist Church, near Black River Falls when Charles Van Schaick took their picture.*

homes with round horizontal logs, once common to Wisconsin, now preserved as landmarks. This type of building was not known in England but was found in Sweden and Finland. It seems to have appeared in America at the time the Finns and the Swedes settled on the Delaware in 1638; and eventually this architectural type of design found its way across the mountains to the Middle Western frontier.[3]

The mother's cabin was generally of small dimensions, from twelve by twelve to twelve by fourteen feet, and contained a puncheon floor—logs split lengthwise. A second room was provided by a low attic which was reached by a ladder or by wooden pegs attached to the wall. This dwelling became the mother's domain although she would fall short in the performance of her duties did not many paths radiate from her door for miles in all directions, since helping her neighbors was one of her many virtues.

ALMOST before the clumsy door was latched, the Indians stopped for

[3]Louise P. Kellogg, "The Society and the State," *ibid.,* 22: 122-123 (September, 1938), quotes from an authority on American architecture.

pork or flour. They liked homemade bread, too. The pioneer mother might receive venison in exchange, but often the "barter" was all on one side. Such an Indian visitor once ate eight large slices of bread and butter, in addition to sausage, and drank three cups of coffee, cups which were not of fine china or of *demi-tasse* capacity. And what did that do to the mother's food shelf? It may have meant a plain potato diet for a long time since the bread supply often depended upon the father's whereabouts, whether he was on his way to the mill or had just returned. Such trips by ox team at times required weeks, especially in late winter when road conditions would have tried the patience of angels. If shortages became critical, borrowing flour from the neighbors was resorted to.

It mattered little whether the mother's house was situated on a well-traveled road, or on a scarcely discernible trail which wound through tall grasses, brightly flowered meadow patches, and dark forests. Almost without exception she became an innkeeper. In sparsely settled areas it had to be so, while in the older sections taverns were conducted on a business basis.

And you ask who crossed over her handhewn sill in those lonely regions? You would be surprised at the variety of boarders and lodgers who stopped for a longer or a shorter period. Especially

A Marquette County farm family, about 1900.

during the late spring and summer months there were many immigrants looking for homes of their own, and a faint light from the little cabin window meant a haven for the travelers in the strange darkness, made grewsome by the howl of the wolf. There were occasional land speculators, moneyed gentlemen, who bought great stretches of virgin land to hold for future profit; there were government surveyors who platted the country so that land could be possessed in better fashion than by "squatting" on it and claiming that priority gave title; there were European travelers who occasionally wrote fantastic accounts after too brief tours of this New America; there were black-robed fathers and circuit riding preachers who received the most cordial welcomes of all.

Why not start along the marshy footpath with a missionary father, tap at several cabin doors en route, and wait for the mother to appear? Father Anthony Gachet of the Capuchin Order, who was ministering to the Menominee on the Keshena Reservation during several years, journeyed to the missionary priest at Green Bay in the summer of 1859, accompanied by a Moravian trader as a companion. They stopped along the way to secure food and lodging. The first day they found a welcome on a little lake-edge farm owned by a half-breed, whose wife was a Menominee. A very good cook, she prepared fish and partridges which she served as the main dish at the evening meal. And there they remained for the night.[4]

The next noon, nearing Duck Creek, they requested food from a Scotch woman, a Catholic convert. First she said "No," with a strong accent, but when she noticed the father's rosary and was assured that he was a priest, she suddenly changed

[4]"Five Years in America," *ibid.,* 18: 196 (December, 1934).

her mind and gave them the best she had.[5] And what that "best" could have been Father Gachet did not say.

Upon their homeward trip they told of their hunger at the cabin door of a good Irish woman, who served them a supper of potatoes and the last piece of pork she had. They protested, but she was not dissuaded. Then she made them a comfortable attic bed with a Negro occupying the same quarters. Serried columns of mosquitoes which had entered through a large hole in the roof made the intense heat more intolerable.[6]

Reading in Father Gachet's journal one senses that he did not become too irritated over existing conditions. He was bigger than stifling heat, humming mosquitoes, and race prejudice. He drenched his soul rather with the fragile beauty of the lady slipper, "delicate rose color, streaked with red rays," as he walked up a hillside, and so impressive was "a magnificent bittern" which rose from a near-by swamp that he noted its flight in his journal.

When one or two uninvited cabin guests arrived, such as Father Gachet and his companion, the mother managed without too much inconvenience, but when a family of a half dozen or more descended upon her, it truly was a case of resorting to the fairy wand. Usually she gave up her own bed, and in addition some of her weary guests slept upon the puncheon floor. When possible, they were made comfortable by the use of straw mattresses, animal skins, or feather beds, untieing their own bundle of coverings if they had not lost them on the way. Sometimes there were no covers, but simply a coming-in out of the cold, the rain, or the dark, when shelter was all that they desired.

Sarah Pratt, a country schoolteacher near Afton, Rock County, and her sister Susannah had come from the East in the 1840's to assuage the desperate homesickness of their married sister, Jane Washburn. Sarah frequently noted in her diary something about the travelers who stopped at the Washburn farm. In April, 1845, Sarah, Susannah, and Jane were hurrying about preparing food for fifty men, who were engaged in a barn raising. Hardly had the supper dishes been removed when a family asked if it were possible to secure lodging. The mother was in great distress from a fractured ankle which had occurred a few miles back when she had jumped from the wagon. It had been one of those extra-busy days, but Mrs. Washburn did not have the heart to turn the newcomers away, especially the suffering mother. The result was that Sarah and Susannah completed their work and spent the night at the home of a friend. The next morning it was up with the sun and back to Jane's to prepare breakfast for helpers and wayfarers.[7]

One of the hospitality centers which welcomed the Norwegians to Wisconsin was the Muskego settlement in Racine and Waukesha counties. There the weary, sea-tossed arrivals sought their countrymen's advice on the selection of lands, or they might ask for financial aid or employment from the leaders of the colony since the "America funds" were often too meager to withstand the battering of the dastardly swindlers found at the debarkation and other transfer points. Late arrivals, delayed by adverse winds upon the Atlantic, might work during the winter months and resume the trek to the farther West early the following spring. But whatever the reason, there was one Norwegian haven as sure as the "Mansions on High."

Among the travelers anxiously awaited at Muskego in 1840 was Even Heg, the father of Colonel Hans Christian Heg of Civil War fame. Sören Bache, residing in the settlement, upon hearing a voice out-of-doors one day, was overjoyed at seeing his good friend at last. Fortunately, Bache's young son had caught a fish, and Even was treated "to a fresh fish . . . and to a cup of tea." When it was time to retire, the bed was moved outside, and other beds were made upon the floor of the little cabin, the unceasing flow of animated talk continuing.[8] Three years after Heg's arrival, the influx of Norwegians was so great that every house in the Muskego colony sheltered from fifteen to twenty persons.[9] An epidemic raging at the time made the housing doubly difficult, but it seems Norwegian mothers found the answer.

The mode of retiring and the flow of talk which continued far into the night was irritating to some of the primitive lodgers. A young Episcopal missionary in Wisconsin during the 1840's wrote to his parents in the East that it seemed barbarous to him at first to retire to a bed in the same room which was the bed chamber of the entire family. "But I am getting somewhat wild myself," he added. An-

[5]*Ibid.,* 197.
[6]*Ibid.,* 199.

[7]A typed copy of Sarah Pratt's diary, 1845, pp. 4, 53-54, is in the Archives, State Historical Society of Wisconsin.
[8]Theodore C. Blegen, *Norwegian Migration to America, 1825-1860* (Northfield, Minnesota, 1931), 128. This was quoted from Bache's diary.
[9]*Ibid.*

A never-ending succession of chores. Feeding the chickens and ducks, near Green Bay, about 1890. A Frederick L. G. Straubel photograph.

other time he wrote that Bishop Jackson Kemper and he "slept eight in a room, and the tattling old woman kept the Bishop awake a long time." [10] The privilege of entertaining the missionary bishop, when the presence of a visiting preacher was considered a special honor, meant that the nervous hostess was doing her best to be hospitable, and in recorded history her unrestrained joy was characterized as "tattling!"

THE pioneer mother led a busy life at any season even though the preparation of extra meals and extra beds became less frequent when the seasonal lull of emigration set in. The space of her first-floor room with its heavy handhewn furniture was at a premium much of the time, but she must have suffered qualms while awaiting the arrival of the church-going crowd. Almost without exception the religious life in the

[10]Charles Breck, *Life of the Reverend James Lloyd Breck* (New York, 1883), 29.

early communities had its beginnings in the little cabins, but mothering and praying had to go on simultaneously if much of the latter was to be done, and few there were who did not believe in its efficacy. Praying could have developed into a fine art among the menfolks while proceeding to the gristmill or to the crossroad trading center behind the plodding oxen—Unonius of the Pine Lake region said he did a great deal of philosophizing while so occupied—but then as now, presumably, they depended upon the women's prayers when days were all stress and strain.

Of course, there were pioneer men at the church services, but the details incident to community worship were in the mother's hands. Her cabin was swept, the alter prepared—frequently a bureau especially beautified was used—all on short notice. When a Catholic father was going her way, or a preacher on horseback swung slowly along the trail, the good news traveled with lightening speed, and shortly there were prayer and admonition and sacrament at her little dwelling.

Prosper Cravath arrived in Walworth County

on May 25, 1840, before his home was completed, and seven days later he recorded that there was preaching at his house on the Sabbath with "quite a respectable assembly about as many as the house would hold."[11] Any day and any hour might take the place of Sunday morning services. In 1837 the settlers in Whiteside County, Illinois, near Wisconsin's boundary, met with the Rev. Amos Miller on Tuesday afternoon at five o'clock, at three-week intervals, again in a little farm home.[12]

When rural areas were opening up, there was a period, often unbelievably long, when the settlers begged for a missionary. While awaiting his arrival, services might be conducted by one of the more gifted men, a type of lay preacher, who read a sermon or excerpts from the Bible. J. K. Meidenbauer wrote to his parents of attending church in the town of Brookfield, Waukesha County, at the Sulzbach farmhouse, with the proprietor taking charge when a traveling preacher was unavailable.[13]

Another layman who held the attention of his audience for two hours, even though he preached in the *Bündernisch* (Swiss cantonal) dialect, was Bartholomew Ragatz. His congregation was composed of Swiss, Yankees, Indians, and other settlers who assembled at his farm home in Honey Creek township, Sauk County. His rich, full voice when he acted as chorister as well as minister transported his listeners, at times numbering several hundred, into other realms. How Mother Ragatz must have thrived on this Sunday sociability since Bartholomew without apology wrote of the many gallons of tears wept by him and his family, when recalling their happy past in Switzerland, during the first winter (1842-1843) in the Middle West.[14]

EVEN though the mother's house was used by the church-going community, it served still another purpose: that of the first country school. She in turn might become a

teacher. These "pay" schools, as they were known, were supported by the parents whose children were enrolled in them. Prior to statehood such a school was conducted in the English Settlement, three miles south of Rochester, Racine County. Edwin Bottomly sent three of his children to school and paid 50 cents a week as his share toward the teacher's salary of $15 a month, for him a rather heavy expense.[15]

During the territorial years the county, the town, and the school district were established as educational units, and each was given the authority to levy taxes in support of schools. Unless the uncertain beginnings of the 1845 Southport experiment be so regarded, there were no free schools during territorial days. Schools "free and without charge for tuition" were provided for in the 1848 constitution.[16]

When all of the planning and most of the savings went into the building of the farmstead, contributing toward the salary of a teacher could not be considered, especially among the foreign born. They felt that religious instruction was essential, and parochial schools met their children's needs, at the same time preserving their native tongue. Consequently they were not greatly concerned in the promotion of the district schools. In fact, when J. W. C. Dietrichson, a Norwegian minister, came to the Muskego settlement in 1844, he discovered that the nearest district school was conducted in a "little, poor log house" and was attended by only a few Norwegian children.[17]

In the Midwestern communities built up by the New England immigrants and other Easterners, the matter of organized schools became of paramount importance almost immediately. Second and third generation Americans could more often afford to educate their children; though they were sent to a home in the settlement at first, a log or frame schoolhouse by the side of the road indicated that young America was on the march.

With buildings completed there loomed the problem of securing a teacher. There were a few curious schoolteachers during the rigorous years who came out from the East "to see for them-

[11]Prosper Cravath diary, May 31, 1840, in the Archives, State Historical Society of Wisconsin.

[12]William F. Sprague, *Women and the West: A Short Social History* (Boston, 1940), 260.

[13]The letter was written in the late summer of 1848 from New Berlin, Waukesha County, to Meidenbauer's parents, who resided in Bavaria, near Nurnberg. John Konrad Meidenbauer Papers, Archives, State Historical Society of Wisconsin.

[14]Lowell J. Ragatz, ed., "Memoirs of a Sauk Swiss," in *Wisconsin Magazine of History,* 19: 209, 220-221 (December, 1935).

[15]An article entitled "English Settlement School," published in the *Burlington Free Press,* July 19, 1945.

[16]William F. Raney, *Wisconsin: A Story of Progress* (New York, 1940), 424. Michael Frank of Southport (Kenosha) was very active in promoting the free-school idea. For a discussion of this movement see Joseph Schafer, *Four Wisconsin Counties: Prairie and Forest* (Madison, 1927), 194-221.

[17]Theodore C. Blegen, *Norwegian Migration to America: The American Transition* (Northfield, Minnesota, 1940), 245.

WHi (X3) 35160

WHi (W6) 27003

*Mary Davison Bradford (left), who at age two tagged along to school in a farmhouse with her
sister, and Kate Deming Wheeler (right), who taught a private school in her father's home in
Kenosha.*

selves," or were motivated by the missionary spirit.
Some of them did not take the schoolroom too seri-
ously, preferring to teach the summer terms when
the "big" boys were unable to attend. There was no
gymnasium, so the young giants found it necessary
to relieve the tedium of reading and writing with
the seasonal "battle of the Superman." Salaries
amounting to $6.00 a month for a two-month term,
or the higher $30 for a three-month term, may have
been an inducement to the "home" girls to leave the
rustic cabin for the adventurous life, and since they
had little to lose, soon chose to raise and command
their own little ones.

The late Mary Davison Bradford, a Wisconsin
educator of eastern parentage, who was reared in
Kenosha County, began her schooling when but a
child of two. Her mother, busy with a family of six,
delegated to ten-year-old Ida the care of little
Mary: rather than give up going to school she took
her tiny sister along. Ida began her school days in
1850 in the large, unplastered living room of a
farmhouse more than a mile from her home and in
unfavorable weather depended upon her father to
furnish the transportation with his wagon and ox
team. The teacher was a girl of the neighborhood

who did a good job in the schoolroom. Mrs. Bradford recalled that a public school, a frame structure, was built in their district in 1851.[18]

Maybe it was her teaching experience, begun in
New York State when she was seventeen, which in
1844 encouraged young Mrs. J. T. Hamilton to
take charge of the first rural school in her locality,
three miles south of Whitewater. She and her husband set up housekeeping in a single room while he
was building their home. Into this room some thirteen or fourteen children trooped. These she taught
while keeping a watchful eye on young Frederic,
less than a year old; her compensation was $1.00 a
week.[19]

Sarah Pratt could not conceive of being deprived
of the little reading and writing knowledge which
she possessed and "often to [o] I feel the need of
more learning," she wrote in her diary.[20] It is not
unusual to find similar remarks made by these
young teachers, though some of them added that

[18]Mary D. Bradford, *Pioneers! O Pioneers!* (Evansville,
[1937?]), 74-75, 89.
[19]J. Talmai Hamilton journal, 86, in the Archives, State
Historical Society of Wisconsin.
[20]Pratt diary, 51-52.

The teacher, far left, and her pupils, including the school clown with his hat over his face, at Weston, 1897.

their work was not difficult since many boys and girls whose parents were foreign born were determined to speak, read, and write the English language, a type of instruction which was performed reasonably well, even with meager training.

Sarah's district demanded a periodic appraisal of her fitness, and her account speaks of taking an eight-mile trip "to be examined."[21] It is common knowledge that some of these examiners knew far less than their candidates, and one can almost believe some such anecdote as when an examiner, thumbing his geography, questioned, "What color is Massachusetts?" Answer, "Blue." Her inspections must have proved satisfactory since she found her pupils in good spirits and became greatly attached to them.[22]

During her short teaching career she "boarded 'round" and walked many prairie miles alone and apparently unafraid. A "neighborhood blessing"

she ministered to the aged, the ill, the overworked, and the dying in much the same way as did the frontier mother. Frail, and troubled increasingly with a cough, she gradually grew weaker and died of tuberculosis in the early autumn of 1847.

One bright-faced Iowan, after being detached from his mother's apron strings for one day, decided that if he became a teacher there would be tragedy. His mother, probably a bit anxious after awaiting his return from his first day at school, asked him how he liked it. Little Linsey-Woolsey replied that if he became a teacher his temper would fly up, killing would follow, and "I'd have to be hung."[23]

[21] *Ibid.,* 34.
[22] *Ibid.,* 59.
[23] Harriet Brown, *Grandmother Brown's Hundred Years, 1827-1927* (Boston, 1929), 97.

THE pioneer mother's school-teaching days were almost forced upon her, but like the Belgian mother's arduous De Pere trips, the experience may have been satisfying in that it provided a "change of motion." If she could have turned to a list of hired girls furnished her by an employment agency, she would have laughed at the idea of being overworked. But, unfortunately, she was dependent almost solely upon the "good-neighbor policy"—all that the words imply—upon the help of an old maid relative in the family (almost non-existent), a grandmother who may have lived with her, or upon the help of her older children.

Comparatively few groups of single women came to America during the first half of the nineteenth century, except for the Irish colleens who arrived with the great exodus from their homeland after the potato famine had left its blight. When these girls landed, the wealthy eastern women employed them immediately, and few of them filtered through to the Middle West. Even in the East the better class was often denied help, and household drudgery meant that things cultural had to be forfeited for a time.[24]

This household problem was observed by Harriet Martineau, who arrived in America in the early fall of 1834, and returned to her home in Great Britain two years later, where she wrote several volumes on the institutions, morals, and manners of the American people. She was greatly concerned about some of the gossipy, wealthy matrons of Boston and New York who took refuge in the boarding houses because of the lack of servants. She was sure that an informed husband would not "willingly expose his domestic peace to the fearful risk" involved.[25]

The Wisconsin mother instead of finding respite in a boarding house was forced to operate one, and sweated more, endured more backache, and added a few more hours to her day. If Providence were extra kind, she might find a hired girl! At the lead mines where help was scarce, an industrious girl could earn $100 a year in addition to her board "either as a domestic assistant, or by serving."[26] The Beloit region could not compete with the lead-region wages, where maids were paid 50 and 75 cents a week in the 1830's and 1840's, a washwoman receiving a shilling a day.[27] Domestics earned from 50 cents to $1.00 a week in the vicinity of Baraboo in the 1850's, the 75-cent rate being commonly paid on a farm to "a good, strong, capable girl, sixteen to twenty years of age," and of course it was understood that gardening and milking were a part of the household tasks. Of women servants, one informant says that they never or very rarely worked in the field but that they took "care of the house, the kitchen, and at most of the stable."[28]

One reads nothing of walkouts and picketing because of the low wages or long hours; instead, the maid probably climbed into the ox-drawn wagon and enjoyed a slow tour to the shopping center where the purchase of a 50-cent hat or a pair of shoes, priced at $1.50, kept her good-natured the remainder of the season.[29]

Carl de Haas, who emigrated from Germany to Fond du Lac County in the 1840's, advised that immigrant girls upon arrival find employment in the large cities where they could demand from $4.00 to $6.00 per month. He found them choosey, however, since "Bachelors are, so to speak, compelled to do their own housework, for a decent girl will rarely go to stay with them."[30]

Some of the wealthy immigrant girls—and there were those who came from excellent homes where servants were employed—lost no time in finding employment. The four daughters of the Norwegian widow, Gunnil Odegaarden, who arrived with their mother when Rock Prairie was just emerging out of the wilderness, were anxious to learn the English language and the American way of housekeeping. Though their mother was well situated, the daughter Gunnil immediately found work.[31] All four of them established homes of their own later.

Since many of the domestics remained in the cities, the newer areas continued their community exchange of labor. And nothing was too menial! A busy mother, who found too much to do when hog-killing time arrived, was greatly relieved when one of her best helpers, a Mrs. McChord of the neighborhood, came over and picked fat from the hog en-

[24]Sprague, *Women and the West*, 67, 222.
[25]*Society in America* (2nd ed., London, 1837), 3: 132-133.
[26]Sprague, *Women and the West*, 75.

[27]H. L. Skavlem, *Skavlem and Odegaarden Families* (Madison, 1915), 158.
[28]"Christian Traugott Ficker's Advice to Emigrants (III)," in the *Wisconsin Magazine of History*, 25: 472 (June, 1942).
[29]Gilson G. Glasier, ed., *Autobiography of Roujet D. Marshall* (Madison, 1923), 1: 105-106.
[30]*North America Wisconsin, Hints for Emigrants by Carl de Haas* (1848-1849), 2 parts in one, translation of 2nd ed. (Fond du Lac, 1943), 57.
[31]Skavlem, *Skavlem*, 158.

trails for leaf lard all day long.[32] This same mother had the help of a "good old maid sister-in-law" part of a year in her Iowa farm home, and she found her far more efficient than an assistant in the region asking $2.00 a week.

When Melinda Weaver was raising her two small children in the vicinity of Waukesha in the late 1830's, she greatly missed her relatives and friends, since there was no one "to be hired for love or money." Milwaukee attracted the young girls, she related, and when there was severe illness the neighbors did the best they could and took turns caring for the patients.[33]

There were frontiersmen who took notice of the endless work their wives performed. When Anson Buttles' wife was struggling with her brood of six small children on a farm near Fox Point, town of Milwaukee, during the Civil War period, her husband came to the rescue to "save the women some hard work." In his diary there was noted for January 16, 1863, the purchase of "a very nice washing machine and clothes wringer," and on March 2, he and little Cephas (not yet six) were promoting a camaraderie that needed no Boy Scout movement to bolster it. "I done all the washing today on the machine and little Cephas wrung the clothes," he wrote.[34]

The wealthier housewives frequently had reason to complain about their servants. There was Caroline Green Strong, for instance. She lived in rather comfortable circumstances at Mineral Point—with the help of a maid some of the time— and was a combination housewife-secretary and a personnel manager. Her days were crowded with the many duties her husband Moses delegated to her while he was away at Madison as a member of the territorial council. Her long communications of the mid-1840's describing her loneliness—they had migrated from Vermont—were concerned especially with the shortcomings of her "men servants," of whom she had employed a long series. The wood was hauled home belatedly, the hay was brought in when the supply was almost gone, and the potatoes were dug long after they should have been. After the 1845 holiday season, Caroline said that Edward, the hired man, spent his time " 'puttering'

WHi (X3) 26600

Caroline Green Strong, a portrait painted shortly after her marriage to Moses Strong; and a photograph taken in her later years.

WHi (X3) 1982

[32]Brown, *Grandmother Brown's Hundred Years,* 122.

[33]*Memories of Early Days* (n.p., 1976), 23. This is a sixty-five-page pamphlet which was published originally in the *Waukesha Plaindealer.*

[34]Typed excerpts from the Buttles' diary (1856-1885, except 1863), are in the Archives, State Historical Society of Wisconsin.

over the chips, and straining water, putting the cattle to bed and tucking them up. He is so slow that he will not get more than one load [of wood] a day in the best of sleighing."[35]

The winter preceding Moses had learned that it was impossible for her to get along with her "house servant." She complained:

"He has so many old batchelor notions & looks so scowling if he is asked to do *little chores and errands. . . . It is quite beneath him to do errands & help little jobs for women folks. . . .* He is *"too old to learn new tricks"*—and I've worried along with him & keep the peace between us, by saying as little for him to do as possible. . . ."[36]

Such were some of the housekeeping troubles of Caroline Strong down Mineral Point way so many years ago; and if her choice of help had not been so limited, she would have sent fewer jeremiads to Moses.[37]

T HE frontier mother could not mourn too much over her help problem; marriage was daily claiming others the same as it had claimed her. She lived in a period when matrimony was enjoying its heyday. The family was the subsistence unit of the primitive years, and it is plain that a husband and wife were an economic necessity to each other; their children in turn filled the role of helpers and were well worth their frugal keep in return for their assistance in the work of the home, the fields, and the forests.[38] Pioneer life brought with it this regrettable child-labor demand, and in the frenzy of farm-making it was accepted as proper and good.

The family unit encountered critical and unpredictable upheavals brought about by puzzling epidemics, by a scarcity of doctors, meager income, and isolation. When the father was taken by death, the widow was usually left with many small children, and she needed someone to assist her in subduing the stubborn enemies of homesteading. Hired workers were as scarce as the money with

which to pay them. If death took the mother, who would cook, sew, spin and weave, process the meat, mold the candles, boil the soap, care for the children, and do the thousand tasks that were her burden? Bachelors were generally in a sad plight, and the records indicate that they found it expedient to hustle around and improve their status since frying salt pork and baking bread were not compatible with cutting-back the forests.

The unmarried girls who left their employment in the eastern cities and the girls who often migrated directly from the old world to the Midwest were therefore not "a drug on the market." Their plans to establish their own homes seldom went awry since there was "a preponderance of men on the fringes of civilization . . . characteristic of all the frontiers of the United States."[39]

Of course, the woman-hunt antedated the arrival of the immigrant girls. History records that Indian consorts of white men and their households of black-eyed offspring were seen frequently during the exploration and fur trade eras. Verbal matrimonial contracts were common among the early French settlers. These Frenchmen believed generally that such contracts were legal; many of the women who obtained husbands in that way likewise thought they were lawfully the wives of the men with whom they lived.[40] James Lockwood, who arrived at Prairie du Chien in 1816, when it housed a village of traders numbering twenty-five or thirty homes, made such early observations.

He also noted while at Green Bay that same summer that this fur trading depot, for the Fox and upper Wisconsin rivers, was inhabited by forty or fifty French-Canadian *voyageurs* who had generally taken as wives women of the Menominee tribe since at that time there was but one local woman who "pretended to be white."[41] These *voyageurs* were unable to continue the hardships of Indian trade, and they and their clerks cultivated, not too successfully, small pieces of land, providing a livelihood for their squaws and half-breed children.[42]

No time was lost in the case of a woman who stepped from a Prairie du Chien ballroom into the loaded canoe of a down-Mississippi trader. Since he ranked her, the proposal exceeded her most cherished dreams, and she immediately paddled

[35]Caroline Strong to Moses Strong, January 8, 1845, in the Moses M. Strong Papers, Archives, State Historical Society of Wisconsin.

[36]*Ibid.,* January 19, 1944.

[37]Moses M. Strong was one of the prominent men of early Wisconsin. His busy life encompassed real estate, railroad, lumbering, and mining interests, and the practice of law.

[38]Solon J. and Elizabeth H. Buck, *The Planting of Civilization in Western Pennsylvania* (Pittsburgh, 1939), 330.

[39]*Ibid.,* 329.

[40]Lockwood, "Early Times and Events in Wisconsin," in State Historical Society of Wisconsin, *Collections,* 2: 110, 176 (1855).

[41]*Ibid.,* 104-105.

[42]*Ibid.,* 105.

down the great river, the haste of her lover not permitting a marriage ceremony. Illegality did not occur to her, even after she and her two children were abandoned a few years later by the once ardent suiter in order that he could take another spouse.[43]

Arriving from Sweden with his bride Charlotta in 1841 after months of ocean travel, Gustaf Unonius in his letters to the homeland newspapers made the domestic help problem appear still more hopeless by advocating marriage. He considered early marriage one of the great advantages of American society. He did not deem it necessary that a prospective husband have a definite occupation or a fixed income in order to marry. A man's "ability to work is the security for an income sufficient to support himself and family," he advised his countrymen.[44]

Carl de Haas, who landed on American soil all trimmed up with a Ph.D. degree from Bonn, frankly admitted that his housekeeping bark was smashing on the rocks in the 1840's, and he discovered that a head crammed full of knowledge did not compensate for an intuitive wife. Things were so rapidly approaching ruin in his farm cabin, he said, that he lost no time in acquiring a mate, and of his whirlwind conquest he wrote, *"Mit dem Freien geht es aber hier sehr rasch, ich gab meiner jetzigen Frau am 26. Januar meinen Wunsch zu erkennen und am 27. Februar waren wir Mann und Weib."*[45] (Courtship progresses rapidly here; I proposed to my present wife on January 26 and we were married on February 27.)

He advised his foreign friends to bring wives along if possible, and in emphasizing the chaotic condition without one, told of the courtship of a well-to-do farmer near Milwaukee, who drove to town and rushed up to an acquaintance, begging his assistance in securing a wife immediately. Together they began a search. The farmer spied a group of immigrants, with a pretty girl among them, following their luggage wagon. He hurried over to them, began conservation, and in a short half hour returned with the young girl on his arm, and asked his acquaintance to accompany them to the justice as a witness. Cheerfully he returned to his farm with his young bride. There was no time

for a honeymoon, and, explained De Haas, "He is happily married!"[46]

Marriage in the New World during the 1840's and 1850's was given consideration even before the girls left the homeland. A concerned brother, living near Waukesha, wrote to his sister in 1851, "One can always marry (here) and at all times; but I do not consider it advisable for you to come to America merely to get married. Far better to become a maid-servant for a while in order to learn American ways and manners, the household, the language. . . ."[47]

The same cheering news was contained in a Stillwater, Minnesota, letter. This settler advised his parents and sisters in Rhine Province, Germany, that even though a girl had no property, if she were well-trained and carried herself well, a very good marriage was in prospect for her since "here no store is set on riches." But he also reminded them that young women who understood housekeeping could earn $10 a month.[48]

The widows, too, were altar bound. An Illinois pioneer whose housekeeper had been with him for a quarter century, rued losing her when she was fifty, to a Mr. W., "having first refused a Monsieur R., an Italian gardner of very polite manners."[49]

Cathedral music, lighted tapers, and misty-eyed mothers resplendent with frail orchids are not a part of frontier wedding stories. A double ceremony which must have caused exciting table chatter in all of the Norwegian cabins at Muskego took place in 1844 when Mrs. Hans Heg's two sisters were married in the Even Heg barn. The emphasis was neither upon music nor lighted tapers but upon the "new home-sawed, oak-framed" structure. John Molee, one of the wedding party, recalled the event many years later. "This was the way Mr. Heg had of dedicating his new barn before he put it to more common use," he said.[50]

Thus the pioneer woman's status as wife and mother was established, and the closely knit family unit with cooperative effort pushed back the forested boundaries. There were ever new recruits, among whom were those who responded to such

[43]*Ibid.,* 176.

[44]George M. Stephenson, ed., *Letters Relating to Gustaf Unonius* (Rock Island, Illinois, 1937), 72n. This letter was written at New Upsala, January 25, 1842, and printed in the Stockholm *Aftonbladet,* May 28, 30, 31, June 3, 7, 9, 1842.

[45]*Nordamerika, Wisconsin; Calumet. Winke für Auswanderer* (Elberfeld, 1848-1849), part 2, p. 32.

[46]*Ibid.,* 32-33.

[47]Nicholas Wertel wrote this letter to his sister who was living in Germany, in the Meidenbauer Papers.

[48]Letter written by F. Schmitz, March 13, 1859, in the Meidenbauer Papers.

[49]Open letter of Richard Flower, Albion, Illinois, June 20, 1820. See Reuben G. Thwaites, ed., *Early Western Travels, 1748-1846* (Cleveland, Ohio, 1904), 10: 128-133.

[50]Rasmus B. Anderson, *The First Chapter of Norwegian Immigration, 1821-1840* (Madison, 1895), 316.

heartening news as "One can always marry (here) and at all times!" The vexing domestic help problem, however, remained unsolved.

MUCH of settlement history comes from the loom of scarcity: there was a scarcity of food, of clothing, of furniture, of cabin space. But the homesteads were teeming with children. Foreign immigration was actuated by the desire to provide the growing family a better way of life, in which cheap land and cheap labor were important factors. "America fever" was especially prevalent among the younger men and it brought them and their families, after hazardous months at sea, to this Utopia. Here they could prove to their satisfaction the fantastic stories of the reported cheap land, and their many children supplied the cheap labor. Aside from being economic assets, numerous children were the fulfillment of the admonition, "Be ye fruitful and multiply"; they were proof of virility and the social standing of the parents, and the "gifts of God" came along unrationed and as a matter of course.[51]

Unimpeachable proof of the fecundity of the frontier mother is contained in the federal manuscript census records. Parents were commonly credited with ten or twelve children, and if the total reached fifteen, in about as many years, it still seemed credible. Whether Irish, Polish, English, German, Dutch, or Scandinavian, every household was generously populating the frontier. In fact many of the early accounts make mention especially of the size of the families.

De Haas made the statment that it was the usual custom in America "that young couples have at least one child a year"[52] which made the log cabin as comfortable as the proverbial "sardine can." Upon his arrival in Wisconsin, accompanied by two of his relatives, De Haas said that his host and wife gave up their bed in the living room to the visitors and slept in the attic, and that at this home, as everywhere else, he found many children.[53] To avoid continued overcrowding the newcomers secured sleeping accomodations at the only inn at Pipe Village.

A writer who spoke of the sterility of American women was reproved by Unonius, who refuted such "nonsense" by relating his observations en route from New York to the West. It was apparent that a bevy of children was attached to every American mother, adding much to the discomfort of his trip.[54] Later he referred to a near neighbor whose household contained fourteen children and commented on the fact that almost all of the homes in his locality were "abundantly blessed with these 'gifts of God.' "[55] Unonius in turn fathered ten children during his seventeen years in America and two more after his return to his native land,[56] of which five died before maturity.

Anson Buttles, of English ancestry, arrived with his parents from the East and settled in Milwaukee township in 1843. After his marriage he and his wife Cornelia Mullie, of Dutch (Netherlands) forebears, lived on a farm near his father and mother and enjoyed somewhat better home conditions than many of those who migrated directly from Europe. The children who played about his farmhouse were not there as an economic asset, since his journal discloses the fact that near-prosperity rode in the Buttles' saddle. He and Cornelia did well in increasing the population figures in Milwaukee County; between 1851 and 1870 there appeared eleven little Buttles.[57]

His diary told of the death by accidental shooting of his brother-in-law Paul Juneau, the son of Solomon Juneau, on August 13, 1858. His sister Olive and her little children were brought home to live. This must have unsettled Grandmother Buttles' housekeeping not a little since she was sixty-four and had reared her family of six. The census lists Olive's children as Anna 10, Laurant 8, Frank 7, Bessie 5, Marian 4, Stoughton 2, and Pauline— a posthumous child—born November 30.[58].

Unless good management and good health were present, mothering a large brood meant that something had to be left undone; the unavoidable hardships of the primitive years had to be dealt with first, at times resulting in filth and vermin.[59] In the great silent hinterland starvation and Indians stalked about, and the mother's knowledge of the use of the musket, kept conveniently over the cabin

[51]R. Carlyle Buley, "Pioneer Health and Medical Practices in the Old Northwest Prior to 1840," in the *Mississippi Valley Historical Review*, 20: 517 (March, 1934).

[52]*North America*, 24.

[53]*Ibid*.

[54]Stephenson, *Letters*, 79.

[55]*Ibid.*, 80.

[56]*Ibid.*, Introduction, 19.

[57]See "Summary of Family History," a typed manuscript which was compiled from the Buttles' diary and is on file with it, in the Anson W. Buttles Papers, Archives, State Historical Society of Wisconsin.

[58]*Ibid.*

[59]Buck and Buck, *Western Pennsylvania*, 489.

Charlotta and Gustaf Unonius with five of their seventeen children, from a photograph loaned by Mrs. M. C. Borman.

door, was as essential to the safety of her growing children as was the planting of potatoes or turnip seeds to assure livelihood during the first winters.

If the tormenting vermin necessitated inspecting little Willie's homespun suit, when matters reached a crisis, no doubt he ran to mother; if the beautifully hand-loomed blankets harbored some evasive "beetles," the well-earned sleep of the over-worked pioneers gave the pest a field day. Even where filth and vermin were present, housekeeping duties allowed little leisure. The older children cared for the younger ones, and the newest starry-eyed addition was assigned to the mother since the time-consuming formulas prepared in sterilized equipment were unknown.

Big Sister glanced into the hand-fashioned cradle occasionally to assist when needed, but even the busiest mother stole a moment to hush her offspring's lusty yelling with playthings which showed inventiveness of the first order. One mother kept her baby from fussing by letting him play with a basket of poppy blossoms, because they were

sleep-inducing! A downy feather glued to the tiny baby's finger with a dab of honey—wild honey—was first-rate entertainment. There were occasions when the mother turned the horse collar over, out in the front yard, and cupped Junior into it where he was as comfortable as he would have been in the latest gadget which some clever inventor might have designed.[60]

Orange juice and "strained this" and "strained that" were not in the cabin cupboard, and as a substitute baby's call for food netted her a bacon rind, sometimes tied to a string.[61] On this, no doubt, she exercised her gums, and if by accident her tid-bit was swallowed, the string was pulled, and watery-eyed Liza caught the rind on her first shiny tooth and began her exercises all over again.

"Be ye fruitful and multiply" brought eventual prosperity. With many children, given a minimum

[60]Brown, *Grandmother Brown's Hundred Years,* 97, 117.
[61]Buley, "Pioneer Health," 516.

Florantha Thompson Sproat, from an oil portrait by her father, Cephas G. Thompson, now in the Society's Museum collections.

of care, a single generation made rapid progress in building a farm out of the wilderness.

As soon as a new occupant, in the long succession, was nestled into the feathery cradle, a naming contest probably was under way. How much excitement, controversy, and mind-changing went into the selection is not on record. However it was done, the census lists were enlightening and hilariously entertaining. Some were beautiful names, others were quaint, and not a few made no sense at all, without a mother's explanation. The custom of naming children for parents and grandparents was as prevalent then as it is today.

How a new little girl, once of southern Wisconsin, could have been punished with the name Ichipene (and then called Ichy by her brothers) will always remain an enigma. Asseline Jackson and Ichipene Spencer could have done mutual condoling. And why wasn't Simpson Bobo christened plain Fred or John? When Colonel and Major Cole arrived, the Civil War was dimly predicted. With such names they should have traveled far, but may have been outdistanced by young Shields, who answered to the name of President. Then there was a Bunos Ayres (whose uncle perhaps had wandered to Buenos Aires), a little Miss Pleasy in the Ames family, and a Cunna daughter in the Beller household.

The Irish mothers preferred the musical Mahala for their violet-eyed little girls—not bestowed as often, however, as Bridget, Mary, and Ellen. Biblical Mary probably was the most popular name listed. Helen, spelled "Hellen," was not uncommon. Other parents favored such names as Bethnel, Freelove, Thankful, Huntington, Angelica, and Relief, which have their counterpart, more recently, in such names as Shirley Kay, Bonnie Lou, Sharon Lee, and Donna Mae.

Perhaps an affidavit should accompany the following list. If anyone is called upon to name a comic radio character, let him scan the huge census volumes and his troubles will be ended. Or he might choose one of these: Elementary Phillip, Preserved Ireland, Anton Pimple, Leberstein Hansom, Desire Liberty, Silence Bell, Hepcke Lipke, America Crank, Marble Bracket, Only P. Outlaw, Ambrose Coffee, Ino Wiser, Remember Bowen, Submit Russell, Stencil Hopp, Honilala Kahal, Wolf Fight, Theophilus Haylet, Hosannah Cower, and Pancratius Dugeisel.

"Wear-well" names which have remained unchallenged in a century or more of competition are such as Fred, Martha, Elizabeth, John, Mary, Louise, and William. The name "Ichipene" is as extinct as the passenger pigeon; it may be inscribed on a disintegrating pioneer tombstone.

MANY of the little Cunnas, Stencils, and Majors could not withstand the rigorous primitive upbringing: the intense summer heat, the penetrating winter cold. The death rate among the infants and younger children was high since the cabins were damp, drafty, and poorly ventilated; food was coarse and unpalatable; milk and water were often contaminated; clothing was insufficient; and income frequently too meager to allow for the visits of a doctor if one were obtainable. Among the many children's diseases entered in the census necrology section were croup, "desentery," teething, cholera, typhoid, and even "consumption," as it was then known.

Again the mother's ingenuity had to meet pioneer medicinal deficiencies, and she did well enough with her knowledge of wild plants, berries, barks, flowers, and roots. These she collected throughout the seasons—gladly assisted by the grandmother—dried and labeled them, and kept them to be used upon short notice. In some of the settlements Dr. Gunn's medical volume was almost as sacred as the Bible and a great blessing during those hard years.

In times of emergency there was no fainting mother—perhaps she had become immunized. She knew she had to rely upon her own knowledge. At times she was a surgeon as well as a physician and fitted and bound together fingers, hanging on shreds; or removed a rusty spike from a foot, washed the wound with hot salt water and hot soda water, and saved the injured member.[62] In the winter of 1836 when a hired man froze his feet while driving hogs from Belvidere, Illinois, to the head of Lake Geneva, no surgeon was at hand. To relieve the patient's suffering the housewife took a pair of shears and amputated several of the frozen toes.[63] If a child's screams told of an unfortunate encounter with a venomous snake, the emergency remedies were applied without a moment's loss of time.

Symptoms baffled the mother at times, and perhaps it was intuitive diagnosis that brought about a cure. These were some of the remedies used and recommended: pleurisy required catnip and pennyroyal; dysentery a poultice of peppermint and tansy leaves; a sore throat and a cold called for a piece of well-peppered fat meat bound around the patient's neck, preceded by an application of goose grease; and mustard and onion poultices, rock candy and whiskey were also considered efficacious. Croup and asthma were conquered with onion and garlic juice while the potent cures for snake bite were applications of salt and gunpowder, crushed garlic juice, or salt and tobacco.[64]

If the illness resulted in death, the infant was placed in a hand-made wooden box. This task was assumed by a woman relative or a good neighbor, who covered the box and lined and padded it with pieces of a sheet, a white dress, or with any material which might answer the purpose. A letter would tell the folks back home of the "passing of little Ambrose," and after a season or two another letter would carry the joyful news that "we have another little boy, which is now the sixth"—or it might have been the twelfth!

When neighborhood women took the place of doctors, who had not yet begun to practice in the backwoods, there was probably one in a region who functioned as a midwife. "Some of these local 'grannies,' as well as the pioneer doctors, were skillful at child delivery; by common sense and practical experience they often overcame the handicap of lack of instruments and other aids."[65] Though accustomed to the strenuous, backbreaking toil in the out-of-doors, too frequent confinement, however, plus hardships and inexpert attention resulted in as many as three mothers in succession coming into many a home.[66]

Dr. P. L. Scanlan, Prairie du Chien historian, wrote of a Sioux woman, by the name of Marie, who early in the nineteenth century practiced among the white residents at Prairie du Chien. Her death in the fall of 1814 was spoken of as "a great loss to this village."[67] Mrs. Charles Menard (Mary Ann La Buche) served as nurse and midwife among the French in the same settlement, and took the place of a physician before the fort was established. Even after regular surgeons were stationed at the military headquarters—when she became a competitor of Dr. William Beaumont—she continued her work in the settlement, herb treatment being among her cures. She often secured excellent results when she took to her home patients whom the physicians were unable to cure. Doctors were jokingly reminded of the superior skill of "Aunt Mary Ann," as she was known in the region.[68]

The absence of physicians at La Pointe, Madeline Island, in the 1830's was of great concern. Mrs. Granville Sproat, the wife of the teacher at the Protestant Mission, wrote to her mother in the summer of 1839 that she had given birth "to a lovely little daughter." The child was stillborn, but had a skillful physician been present she believed he might have saved the infant. A few weeks later she continued the letter and reported that Mrs. Sherman Hall—whose husband was the minister at the same mission—had become a mother the last of January, "when only Mr. Hall and myself were

[62]Brown, *Grandmother Brown's Hundred Years*, 157-158.
[63]*History of Walworth County* (Chicago, 1882), 337.
[64]Buley, "Pioneer Health," 505-506.

[65]Madge E. Pickard and R. Carlyle Buley, *The Midwest Pioneer: His Ills, Cures, & Doctors* (Crawfordsville, Indiana, 1945), 32.
[66]*Ibid.*
[67]*Prairie du Chien: French, British, American* (Menasha, 1937), 199; "Anderson's Journal at Fort McKay, 1814," in State Historical Society of Wisconsin, *Collections*, 9: 241 (1882).
[68]Scanlan, *Prairie du Chien*, 199; Lockwood, "Early Times," 125-126.

The Sauk Center family of Wilhemina and Herman Bernard Niermann II made ready for the photographer, about 1900.

assistants, he being midwife and I nurse. . . . Mrs. Hall is very feeble and has been so ever since her confinement."[69] Though families were large, the mortality of infants whose mothers had no professional prenatal care was likewise great.

The then incurable "consumption" attacked families with viciousness, and one member after another lingered and passed on. Men, women, and children, of all ages, filled the cemeteries, victims of this puzzling disease. The number of children bereft of their mothers was legion. One of the most complete case histories was found in the diary entries of Sarah Pratt, who was afflicted with the dis-

ease. Hers was an almost day-by-day account, the sufferer completely debilitated toward the close of the journal.

The epidemics of smallpox, typhoid, and cholera left regions desolate; the recurring fever and ague, pneumonia (known as lung fever or inflammation of the lungs), dropsy, dysentery, rheumatism, and mental disorders were other illnesses which left homes motherless, or unavoidably neglected.

Fever and ague sometimes is recalled in the reminiscences and letters of the early period as a disease that almost shook the doors of the cabins off their hinges. Not because it was as vicious and fatal as were the cholera epidemics, but because of the long and debilitating sieges which appeared as reg-

[69]"La Pointe Letters," in the *Wisconsin Magazine of History,* 16: 89-90, 93 (September, 1932).

ularly as the seasons. It was dreaded for its tenacious habits. One historian says that fever and ague was so common that it was considered as something to be expected on the frontier, like hard work. "He ain't sick, he's only got the ager," was the attitude taken by the settlers.[70]

The disease was described as beginning with yawning and a feeling of weariness, then the chills appeared, growing worse until the teeth chattered, and the victim resembled "a miniature earthquake in the chimney corner." Blueness of the fingernails developed and after about an hour the person afflicted began to feel somewhat normal. Then followed a high temperature with severe pains in the head and back. When profuse perspiration set in the patient knew that his attack was ending. There were several kinds of fever and ague; some victims had combined chills and fever each day, or on alternate days, and some every third day. Though the attacks seldom were fatal, they were so enervating that the patient was unable to resist more serious illnesses.[71] During those weeks, sometimes months, the farm and household work might be at a near standstill, or done intermittently.

This puzzling "malarial" illness, also known as "autumnal fever," arrived in earnest during the torrid July and August days and continued through September, becoming less troublesome during the months following. It was noted to be particularly prevalent in the bottoms. Among its supposed causes were the miasmatic swamp vapors; vegetable decay in the fall; poor locations of wells; and damp, dark, crowded and unsanitary cabins.[72] The disease was conquered in time, especially after the swamps and lowlands were drained and were added to the tillable areas. Improvements in living conditions, with better constructed houses, may have been a factor in eradicating this illness.

In the fall of 1846 the disease seemed to have been especially prevalent, Mrs. J. T. Hamilton's family, in the vicinity of Whitewater, began suffering with the fever and ague shortly after she gave birth to Philena. Her sister, visiting at the home, was the first to be attacked, then her father fell ill, next her two-year-old Freddie and her mother. Two young women, both of whom were in poor health, were called in to aid with the house work. When December arrived the father had recovered, and when spring rolled 'round, the mother had finally "slain her dragon." "It was a time of general sickness throughout the country," the young husband wrote in his journal, but newborn Philena went through it unscathed.[73]

In September, 1851, shortly after the birth of a son, Mrs. Hamilton became ill with the ague, as she thought, but was unable to cure it with the usual home remedies. A physician was called but he, too, was unsuccessful, and after a few weeks she succumbed to "Interic [enteric] Fever of a Typhoid character," according to Hamilton's record.[74]

Writing of the same region, Prosper Cravath also noted the sickly season of 1846, with two to four Norwegian families living together, sometimes in a one-room house. In these crowded quarters from three to six ailing persons were barely able to move. He wrote that "in a single room, there were, at the same time, six lying around the sides of the room, unable to rise; all with a dish of water at their side and a rope extended from a joist overhead in which to rest their head when they drank, there being only two small girls, about seven and ten years old, able to render assistance. In the village, few escaped the plague." Some sat huddled outside, yellow and haggard, sunning themselves, anxiously looking at their fingernails; others dragged about, seeking sympathy.[75]

Ague or no ague, one husbandman followed his plow! A workman told Tosten, the son of Abram Holverson, that one day when big, barefooted Abram was breaking sod, he was attacked by a severe ague; the driver was compelled to stop the oxen, and Abram "lay down in the furrow to shake it out." When he felt better, the powerful man arose, the driver "gee-hawed" the oxen, and breaking sod was resumed. This may have been a unique performance since, with his magnificent physique, it was said that Abram did not know the meaning of the word "hardship."[76]

It is evident that additional burdens were assumed by the frontier mother when this miasmatic creature crept in from the swamps. If she were spared from the attacks, she would have to carry the work of other family members since every home was visited ruthlessly.

THE howl of the wolf, the warfaring Indian, the forest fire, and the food

[70]Buley, "Pioneer Health," 499-500.
[71]Ibid., 499.
[72]Sprague, Women and the West, 75.
[73]Hamilton journal, 87.
[74]Ibid., 98.
[75]Prosper Cravath and Spencer S. Steele, Early Annals of Whitewater, 1837-1867 (n.p., 1906), 76.
[76]Skavlem, Skavlem, 160.

shortage were all dreadful monsters encountered by the mother, but at least they were combatable. The most fearsome of all was the sinister cholera scourge, which appeared at its worst in 1832, 1849, and at short intervals during the early 1850's.

Of all the heartbreaking memories that came to the pioneers, the blackest were probably those of the cholera visitations. It is a gruesome tale: the loss of husband, or wife, or children, or of entire families, to say nothing of aging parents and more distant kinfolk. There were times, too, when immigrants were separated by this hideous specter while crossing the sea or while steaming up the Mississippi to find their new homes. In a strange country, unable to speak the English language, often without funds beyond the cost of transportation or at most a season of frugal living, these travelers when face to face with the terrifying plague must have regretted their stout resolutions made some months earlier. The resulting grief was so poignant that when madness came, as it sometimes did on the frontier, one can well believe that the grief over pestilence was a contributing factor.

An eastern newspaper editor was as baffled at the appearance and relentlessness of these epidemics as were the early physicians at the fatality of the disease. The editor tried to help his bewildered readers by printing some instructions and warnings in these words, "If your neighbor is sick and you can be of any help, visit him. If he *dies*, bury him. If you can be of no *help*, keep away."[77] The mother of the frontier mindful of the paths that radiated from her cabin door knew that where there was suffering, she was needed. She went; she did not always return.

Cholera was first brought from Europe to Quebec and Montreal in the summer of 1832. From there it was carried to New York and spread south and west over the continent. The troops, under General Winfield Scott, who were detailed to Wisconsin in order to assist in subduing the Black Hawk War disturbances brought it from the East by way of the Great Lakes. One of his soldiers was attacked on a transport, and shortly after the troops at Detroit and Chicago were victims. There was panic, and the deserting soldiers caused the plague to appear in remote posts.[78]

Dr. William Beaumont, who was stationed at Fort Crawford, came in contact with the disease and quieted the inhabitants. His explanation as to its fatality was that "the greater proportional numbers of deaths in the cholera epidemics are . . . caused more by fright and presentiment of death than from the fatal tendency of the disease."[79]

The 1849 newspapers published at New York, Cincinnati, St. Louis, Toledo, Detroit, Chicago, and in the cities of Iowa and Wisconsin, all were broadcasting stories of this ravaging epidemic which appeared especially active among the newly arrived immigrants and the poorer classes. Editors discussed its puzzling nature and printed the reports of the health officials which showed the increase or decrease in the number of deaths, at intervals, but the cause remained an enigma.

And who has not read in the Wisconsin pioneer letters and diaries of the tragic deaths of the gold-seekers on the overland route to California in 1849? The wagon trains passed newly made graves by the score, and many of the victims may have belonged to the large band enumerated as "mysterious disappearances." No word ever reached their families.

Seventeen-year-old Lucius Fairchild, who later became the state's governor, traveled out on this trail, and his letter written at St. Joseph, Missouri, on April 23, 1849, must have brought uneasiness to his family at Madison. In it he told of his recovery from "an attack of that great plague cholera. I had it on the boat near St. Louis but I checked it in time although I was alarmed some. . . . I thought of home when I was so sick I could hardly stir and how lonely it was to be among strangers and sick."[80]

John Molee described this same summer as the "awfulest" he had ever experienced when devastation was rampant in Muskego settlement. "There were, at one time, only seven families all well, so that they could get away to help their neighbors," he wrote. Molee and his brother, with the use of their ox team, had all they could do to remove the dead from the homes to the cemetery "while others dug the graves. . . . We simply rolled a white sheet around the dead, unwashed and unshaved; and then we placed him or her into a rough board box." The burial ground selected was named "In-

[77]*Milwaukee Sentinel and Gazette,* July 2, 1849, from the *New York Journal of Commerce.*

[78]See biography of Dr. William Beaumont in the *Dictionary of American Biography* (New York, 1929), 2: 107; also Deborah Martin, "Dr. William Beaumont," in the *Wisconsin Magazine of History,* 4: 277-278 (March, 1921).

[79]Martin, "Beaumont," 278-279.

[80]Joseph Schafer, ed., *California Letters of Lucius Fairchild* (Madison, 1931), 8.

The Field family cemetery headstone, New Diggings, 1957, photographed by Dan Porter.

dian Hill," and while the Molees were so engaged, they expected to be stricken at any moment. "We stood by our post of duty like true soldiers of peace, live or die."[81]

Historian H. G. Gregory recorded that in the summer of 1850 "at one time 18 bodies lay on the ground awaiting burial in the Catholic cemetery" at Milwaukee, but he stated that after 1854 cholera did not become epidemic in that city again.[82] Rasmus Anderson lost his father and brother in the Koshkonong region in 1850 and noted the "great depredations" wrought by the disease in that area.[83]

In recalling the severe cholera siege at Milwaukee in the summer of 1851, Amherst Kellogg quoted the Rev. W. S. Miller, a Methodist minister of that city, as saying, "To attend six funerals a day and to visit twice that number of sick persons was not an unusual experience. To meet a well man at a burial one day and to attend his funeral the next or the day following was not an infrequent occurrence." He also related the demise of the Methodist presiding elder of the Milwaukee district, the Rev.

Elihu Springer, who "was attacked at Oconomowoc at three o'clock in the morning of the twenty-second of August, and though medical aid was called at once, he died at six o'clock in the evening before his wife could reach him from Milwaukee. . . ."[84]

A letter in a Swedish homeland newspaper contained the observation that Chicago was healthful in the summer of 1852 until a detachment of Swedes arrived. In this crowded city, of eleven adults and fifteen children who lived in a five-room house, fifteen died in one week, and six children were orphaned. "This has been going on for the last two months," the editor was informed.[85]

[81]Anderson, *Norwegian Immigration*, 321-322.
[82]*History of Milwaukee, Wisconsin* (Chicago, 1931), 2: 1136.
[83]Anderson, *Norwegian Immigration*, 390.
[84]"Recollections of Life in Early Wisconsin," in the *Wisconsin Magazine of History*, 8: 110 (September, 1924).
[85]Stephenson, *Letters*, 132-133. Letter written at Chicago, September 20, 1852, to the editor of the *Aftonbladet* and published February 3, 1853.

Correspondents also told of the distress in the little settlements. In an open letter written on August 8, 1854, at Port Washington and published in the Milwaukee *Daily Sentinel* the following day, the news was broadcast that cholera had been raging in that village for three weeks. In spite of all the medical skill that could be obtained, whole dwellings were left desolate. The same paper on August 16 printed an item on the seriousness of the visitation at Sauk City where many deaths occurred.

Thirty-six succumbed to the disease between July 3 and 17, 1854, in the Rock County Norwegian community of whom two were Americans.[86] It was the summer that Widow Gunnil Odegaarden, that blessed mother of the frontier, then living with her son-in-law in Newark township, was carried away by the plague. Her aid and advice to those in distress had always been given freely. Though small and frail, she was characterized as resourceful and energetic, possessing those qualities that make up the ideal pioneer. Halvor Skavlem in telling of this great-hearted woman's death, said, "She was the sixth and last victim at Mr. Holverson's home. Consecutively for six days Mr. Holverson made a trip to the cemetery with a cholera victim for burial."[87]

The mother's fears and fortitude must have been strangely intermixed during these grievous times. She lived dangerously, days without end, but a pioneer minister explained her immunity to the plague in this beautiful and simple thought, "She must have been surrounded by angels."[88]

I N addition to the hardships already enumerated, an especially menacing one, still unaccounted for, was loneliness. It must have taken all the self-control the mother could muster to appear stout-hearted. When her days were the busiest, nostalgia may have lost its acuteness to return with vengeance when she snatched a moment here and there to think and feel. And sometimes indulgence in the thought of her loneliness and the monotony of her Herculean struggle brought on prolonged mental illness.

One historian wrote that the immigrant's mind "was sensitive to the pain and loss inseparable from migration; and as he mulled over his experi-

ence he thought much about the land he had come from."[89] The fjords of Norway, the mountains of Switzerland, the heaths of Scotland, the valley of the Rhine, the sparkling lakes of Ireland, and the dykes and fertile patches of the Low Country, all were disturbing elements in the Americanization process. Would it not seem that of the newcomers the foreign-born mother, who could speak only her native tongue, suffered the greatest pain over separation, the adjustment often not completed during her lifetime?

In America there was the tendency to form compact foreign settlements, and the native tongue continued to be used among these exclusive European groups.[90] The mother, of course, conversed with her friends and family in the language she was accustomed to, though her children often progressed rapidly in learning to speak English.[91] The feeling of isolation must have increased as her children hurried along the road of Americanization ahead of her. Her meager social life, at most a visit with her kinfolk and worship at the native-language church, with some opportunity for news exchange, would do little to increase her fluency of English speech.

The men of the family had dozens of contacts off the farm while she could do her housekeeping year in and year out, without the necessity of acquiring an intermediate language. A necessary spoke in the wheel of the subsistence unit, she seldom needed to go beyond the boundaries of her wilderness homestead unless she chose to do so. But the father and his sons had to make immediate contacts upon arrival—and natural enough in the light of Old World prerogative. Hardly had they lugged their chests and bundles off the Great Lakes or the Mississippi River steamboat when the necessity of conversation challenged them to a new kind of speech. A visit to the land office, room and job hunting, the purchase of oxen and a vehicle, later neighborhood cabin and barn raisings, threshing, delivering logs and grain to the mills, bartering for tools and the few necessities not produced on the farm, such business required more than the sign language, though gesturing probably helped to initiate the intermediate way of speech. And so the "cosmopolitan" outlook was acquired by the father and his sons, and the crude hyphenated-language put in use by them far sooner than by the mother, long snug in her own isolation. And it was not difficult for them to

[86] *Milwaukee Daily Sentinel,* July 27, 1854.
[87] Skavlem, 160.
[88] N. N. Rönning, *The Saga of Old Muskego* (Waterford, Wisconsin, [1943]), 46.

[89] Blegen, *American Transition,* 80.
[90] *Ibid.,* 73-74. Blegen's chapter 3, "Language and Immigrant Transition," 69-99, is a fascinating account.
[91] *Ibid.,* 73, 81.

fall back momentarily into the old way at the gatherings of their "clan," at the church services, or around the kitchen table.

Letters written by the foreign-born rural settlers were a happy link with their native land. Filled with advice to future immigrants on farming methods or employment opportunities in the new country, these messages were carefully composed by the father. When writing to his parents or brothers, more personal items might be included, such as the size of the first litter of pigs, the purchase of a second cow, and the condition of his purse—more often than not, completely deflated! If a part of the page were not filled, the mother might add a paragraph or two. And can there be much doubt that to relieve her pangs of loneliness she was glad to "pour out her heart" in a few postscript lines? Postage rates were too high to permit lengthy letters, as a rule, and often there were no postscripts from the mother. If by chance a group leader—a propagandist—or some acquaintance should return to the homeland, he gladly delivered communications to the relatives of the immigrants.

The indifference of one man to his wife's possible adjustment to the pioneer environment, incident to leaving the family and friends, may only be a "story," but it has a kernel of truth in it. Asked whether she would not suffer from loneliness on the frontier, he replied, "Wall, if she does, I expect I shan't mind it much, if she keeps it to herself."[92]

Probably she did keep it to herself, in the hope that the time would come when she would recross to visit the distant place of her birth. It is doubtful whether she really permitted herself to believe such daydreams. At least they acted as a temporary antidote. Or if she could control herself no longer, she

[92]Sprague, *Women and the West*, 69.

A strong, proud Black River Falls area family, photographed by Charles Van Schaick.

would one day break her silence and her inhibitions would cease from then on. Such was the experience of John Molee, who left this record, "My wife was often sorry she came to the wilderness of Wisconsin for her father had a fine farm and servants." The "America fever" had brought her and her family to this country.[93] The wish to return to the home that she had once known could never have been fulfilled completely since her mother and a sister had been buried at sea.

There was less gloom if the mother could tell another woman of her lonely feelings, but often there was no one to sympathize. Jacob Bale and his family settled in Kentucky in 1797. Shortly thereafter he visited Holland to attend to his wife's inheritance. She and her young children remained in the wilderness of Kentucky since someone had to manage the farm and the mill. Almost two years Sapphia Bale carried on in this sparsely settled region and then one day while she was baking bread she glanced out of the window. "There comes Jacob," she commented to someone and continued with her baking.[94] Even affection "flew out of the window" in this farm-making struggle. " 'Will it work?' men asked in choosing tools, and perhaps wives."[95]

Katharine Börner Hilgen, of Cedarburg, wrote of her loneliness to her brother and sister-in-law at Charleston, South Carolina. It was in the late summer of 1846 when she described her beautiful flowers, and the admiration given them by passers-by, which gave her much pleasure, but still she was sad. "If I only had a few good true women friends, I would be entirely satisfied. Those I miss." She sent greetings to her sister also and expressed the desire that the sister come to Wisconsin, and exclaimed, "I would like to spend a day with you all."[96] Near the holiday season of that year she again sent a communication to the same relatives, rejoicing over the prospect of her brother's removal to Wisconsin. "Then we will live our lives together in happiness." A short note to her sisters Anna and Meta contained the wish, "I hope you will come here too so that we will all be together again."[97] Life's mosaic had been disturbed, and Katharine was concerned about fitting the pieces into place.

Think of Fredrika Bremer, the Swedish traveler in America during 1849-1850, doing all in her power to inspire her young hostess "with better feelings toward the country, and a better heart!" Her subject was the pretty nineteen-year-old wife of a Norwegian minister in the Koshkonong community, who had recently come to America. Fredrika included Madison in her tour, and on a fall day in 1850 she was driven to this Norwegian rural community in order to observe the immigrants' farm life. She found the lonely wife in a log cabin, her husband away on business; she was "sick at heart for her mother, her home, and the mountains of her native land, nor was she happy in this strange country." During the night there was a terrific thunderstorm and torrential rains, which frightened the young woman and she "sighed over the life in 'this disagreeable country.' "[98]

There was one energetic frontiersman, Bartholomew Ragatz, who developed a large Sauk Prairie farm, arriving in 1842. When evening came, he found much pleasure in looking over his many acres, and would exclaim exultantly, "It is ours, every bit ours!" This thought brought him contentment, but not so his wife. "She never complained," he said, but "somehow, her courage often failed her," and she could never bring herself to believe that the almost uninhabited prairie would one day be the place of many homes. The mill, the comfortable house as well as the beloved Alps which vanished in the misty distance as the travelers were outward bound were left forever. She never saw them again. Even with her many children, some of them adults upon reaching Wisconsin, and the good way of life which was provided for her, the change from her little European hamlet to the isolated and almost unpopulated prairie of Wisconsin left a nostalgic ache in her heart.[99]

Some immigrant families started on the trip to America in fine spirits, but unforeseen tragedies brought loneliness before they even reached their destinations. When Mrs. T. S. V. Wroolie was a small child, she crossed the Atlantic from Norway with her father, mother, and three other children. She recalled in her "Memories" that when leaving Quebec her father fell through the hatchway of the top deck to the bottom of the ship which resulted in his death. The crew took charge, and when the mother was allowed to search for the $400 which

[93]Anderson, *Norwegian Immigration*, 317.
[94]Ida L. Bale, "Three Generations of New Salem Pioneers," in the *Journal of the Illinois State Historical Society*, 37: 352-353 (December, 1944).
[95]Buck and Buck, *Western Pennsylvania*, 490-491.
[96]"German Pioneer Letters," in the *Wisconsin Magazine of History*, 16: 436-437.

[97]*Ibid.*, 439.
[98]*Homes of the New World* (New York, 1853), 1: 631-633.
[99]Ragatz, "Memoirs," 189-190.

was sewed inside of the father's clothing, it was missing. The body was removed, and the family never knew the place of the father's burial.[100]

This mother, now without money and the care of her four small children, depended upon the generosity of friends, whom she had learned to know en route. Delayed in crossing the Atlantic the travelers arrived late, and the relatives who had come to meet them at La Crosse, had returned home. So the penniless, discouraged widow accompanied several of her traveling companions into Minnesota, where some of her children were put into private homes, and she was employed by the day, working most of the time in the fields. The bitterness of her experience in a strange land was short-lived. She died about thirteen years later.[101]

The American-born mother added her experiences in loneliness to the foreign-born, and the records, of whatever kind, must have been moistened with her tears. A young bride, Mrs. Elizabeth T. Baird, arrived from Mackinac Island to make her home at Green Bay in September, 1824. In order to reach her neighbors, a quarter of a mile away, she had to pass through a dark woods. Henry S. Baird, who practiced law, made a two-mile trip on horseback each morning in order to reach his office. Elizabeth, in this Indian country, stayed alone during the day, and in her "Reminiscences of Life in Territorial Wisconsin," wrote, "That I shed many tears I cannot deny." The isolation of this military post, though pleasant in a social way, did not make up for the paucity of letters from "the dear old island," only two being received during the year, one in winter, another in the spring.[102]

Whether the mother lived at a military post or at a lonesome mission, her separation from the family circle and the few communications which were received made some days unbearable. Florantha Sproat, the wife of the mission teacher at La Pointe, was longing to see her people in faraway Massachusetts. She had said good-bye to them several years earlier, and when the missionary box arrived from the East in 1842 it gave her both pleasure and pain. "When I came to look for letters and tokens of remembrances from home and finding only yours and Elvira's containing only a few lines, and no news, I felt pained and disap-

WHi (X3) 24206

Elizabeth Therese Baird, who came to Green Bay in 1824 as the young bride of Henry S. Baird.

pointed for I had been waiting with fond hopes of great pleasure half the year not hearing from home the time."[103]

In a letter to her family in the form of a diary, written in the spring of 1842, she explained that when a traveler arrived on the mainland, he would start a fire; when smoke arose, an islander would take a canoe and cross over for him. At this time they had been expecting the men who had been sent for the mail, a distance of between four and five hundred miles through the uninhabited wilderness. "You have no idea of our feelings at such a time. . . . The mail has arrived being many [let-

[100]"An Immigrant's Memories," in *La Crosse County Historical Sketches,* Series 7 (La Crosse, Wisconsin, 1945), 77-78.

[101] *Ibid.,* 78-80, 82.

[102]State Historical Society of Wisconsin, *Collections,* 15: 205, 209, 216 (1900).

[103]"La Pointe Letters," 93-94. This letter was addressed to her mother, Mrs. Cephas Thompson, Middleborough, Massachusetts, October 10, 1842.

ters] for others and none for me. My disappointment is great." She must have wept, for a great many months had elapsed since she had had news; several weeks later she was made happy by receiving a letter from her mother.[104]

Since Florantha was in poor health, a plan had been considered to send her east to return in the spring of 1843 with the Rev. Mr. Hall, who was the missionary at La Pointe. This time there must have been disappointment in the old-home circle, too, when information came that their daughter had dropped the proposal. The board had not been informed concerning it, and "the prudential committee would think it strange," was the reason given.[105]

Loneliness was an integral part of the mother's

frontier battle. On the whole there was no turning back. As the years wore on, there was a mellowing of the feeling of loss caused by migration; as the region increased in population with the arrival of more of her relatives and acquaintances, and the narrow trails became well-traveled roads, as her children's children brought additional responsibilities, loneliness took a minor place in her life, or at least it was accepted passively. In the midst of an inquisitive and new generation she knew she must live still more courageously. There was no place for tears.

And now this brief story of the Wisconsin frontier mother has been retold. Admirable in her possession of courage, initiative, and ingenuity—intermingled with fear and loneliness—she must for all time stand as a symbol of the early day. Selfless in her doing, she contributed a significant part in the creation of "a goodly heritage."

[104] Ibid., 201-202.
[105] Ibid., 209.

WHi (W6) 11232

"The Pioneer Woman," a statue by Bryant Baker, near Ponca City, Oklahoma.

Lillian Krueger was a researcher and writer for the State Historical Society for twenty-seven years. A 1928 graduate of the School of Journalism of the University of Wisconsin-Madison, she began work in 1929 at the Society as a research and editorial assistant to Joseph Schafer, the director. Between 1929 and 1948 she edited the Society's books and compiled the *Proceedings*. In 1942 she was named assistant editor of the *Wisconsin Magazine of History*, progressing to associate editor in 1945 and to managing editor in 1949, a position she held until her retirement in 1956. She wrote numerous articles for the *Magazine*, as well as for other historical journals and various newspapers. She was also the author of *A Centennial History of the First Evangelical United Brethren Church of Madison, 1855-1955*. Ms. Krueger died in Milwaukee on September 4, 1970.

5000-3J00041-80